Ben Ray

To Lona

Keep reading - the world

After the Poet, the Bar

needs more poetry!

Ben Ray

Indigo Dreams Publishing

First Edition: After the Poet, the Bar
First published in Great Britain in 2016 by:
Indigo Dreams Publishing
24, Forest Houses
Cookworthy Moor
Halwill
Beaworthy
Devon
EX21 5UU

www.indigodreams.co.uk

ISBN 978-1-910834-18-3

British Library Cataloguing in Publication Data. A CIP record for this book can be obtained from the British Library.

Designed and typeset in Palatino Linotype by Indigo Dreams.
Cover; 'Monnow Bridge' by David Day
Printed and bound in Great Britain by 4edge Ltd.

Papers used by Indigo Dreams are recyclable products made from wood grown in sustainable forests following the guidance of the Forest Stewardship Council.

for my family

Thank you to Indigo Dreams Publishing for giving me this fantastic opportunity. Many thanks to Nancy Campbell, Jonathan Edwards and Rory MacLean for their kind testimonials. Thank you to Jon and Kate Bowra, for being there to help at the last hurdle. And finally, thank you to my friends and family for all their support and encouragement: especially to Mum and Jasper, who listened to endless drafts endless times.

After the Poet, the Bar is Ben Ray's first full collection

Web: https://benraypoetwordpress.wordpress.com/

CONTENTS

After the Poet, the Bar

**Letter from Fletcher Christian, Founder of the Pitcairn
Community Following the Mutiny on the Bounty, to his old
Classmate William Wordsworth**

Dear Bill,
we've come a long way- as many months as miles.
Can you hear this over the ocean? Do you remember us?
The waves have washed the years smooth
since you and I were in that classroom together:
the Cumbrian sun filtered like strained tea
through the glass that separated us from the sky.
Remember how we both talked of escaping?
Of releasing our sleeping selves into the wide awake world –
stretching and stepping out of our footprints
embedded generations deep in cold Northern soil.
We were going to write our names on our children, our friends,
on the very sun that had enticed us outside
until the whole world knew who we were
and the heavens rang with the knowledge
that we were there. That we existed.
And now, at night, even half a world away,
I can see your language rising up through the earth.
I have swapped poetry for parakeets,
there are no daffodils here – all verdant,
aggressive green, shouting out to the crystal Pacific.
The pace of the path is the only metre I know,
measuring the steps that circle my coastal kingdom
and the rhyme and rhythm of my days
are counted in steady stanzas of surf and salt spray.
And yet sometimes, if I throw my name into the air
and hear Pitcairn whisper it softly back to me,
feeling it sinking slowly into every gap and gully,
your voice seems to mingle with mine.

Rain Clouds over Edinburgh

There is a moment,
just before the beginning,
where the light slides up the walls
to avoid oncoming traffic
and is draped boldly over buildings
until it is one bright, burning canvas
with house fronts sketched loosely on
ready to be washed away
by the incoming ending.
There is a moment,
as the very air breathes slowly in
and the darkness of the sky above
accentuates the bright aliveness below –
and the whole unfurls lily-like
begging for the sky's caresses.
There is a moment,
just before the world collapses inwards,
on all the corbels, the towers,
the rooftops, the doorways,
the pub fronts, the bus stops,
the cobbles, the church spires,
the gnarled and twisted trees
that lean on the fences of Tron Kirk:
when all the world undresses
and waits for the wash of the rain.

New Landscapes

The mountains are beautiful today.
The road traces their shadows
like trailing fingers through water –
empty skies on an empty day.
But it may only be because
the mountains lead to Wales
to you. If you wanted, I would roll the skyline up,
pack away the card-deck of hills and valleys
and bring them to you.
(I'm sure the car is big enough.)
We could watch the sea lap against the contour edges
of a new, homemade landscape.

A Study in Urban Botany

On the bridge behind the Tescos
sprouting out from the cracks of the pavement
there's a small, delicate blue plaque
pinned tastefully to the railings. It reads:
Geranium Robertianum flowered here
from June to October 2014.
The railings have been lovingly repainted
and the pavement has been recently swept –
there isn't a weed in sight.

In the doorway of a McDonalds
two homeless men crouch on plastic bags
discussing where best to spend the night.

Origin of Species

Show me your home.
Show me your origins, your roots, that alpha aspect
that leads into the beta of beyond: that bond,
where the almost visible stasis of the place is
a familiar voice in a crowd. In the top cupboard of the mind,
a well-handled shoebox of glittering, lazy Sunday mornings
to be picked up gingerly, gazed at, put back softly.
Show me the land your feet grew out of.
The earth, the soil that sustains you, and that retains too
those first, fleeting moments,
imprints on sand that water has drained through.
The place where your footprints
are always waiting for you on the beach –
the most comfortable shoes you own.
Look – though you've grown, the sea is there to remind you
things are still the same. Tides, wash, spray, swash
the long-shore drift of life that will always pull you back here.
Show me the place that shapes
the contours of your unconscious
and one day soon, hopefully, I will show you mine;
safe haven, bolt hole back to the base of your being
where the air is freeing, seeming to fit your insides
snugly when you breathe in. Look,
though you are not mirrored exactly in these rocks any more,
though you have left, gone elsewhere – the land doesn't care.
The stones on the beach still recognise your reflection.

Vocational Clothing
(With thanks to Jon Bowra)

When going out dining
Mozart thought it was neat
to show off his new work
and wear a three piece suite.

Lunch with Larkin

It is possible to fill an empty room with voices:
at an empty table, I have Larkin propped by my plate.
Fork blindly stabs at salad – the hand that holds it
is attached to a mind attending the Whitsun Weddings:
'when all the advice and confetti had been thrown...'
Until now I am again at my desk, Larkin sitting on the shelf
and a pen in my hand. The paper leers upwards.
There are more birds now. They dart and scurry
to and fro outside my window, diving and landing
like promises of warm-hugged days on the grass
and the slowing of time to an August crawl.
I glance at Larkin. He looks steadily back.
The paper watches us watching one another.
'A sense of falling, like an arrow-shower sent out of sight...'
Beyond me, the birds chatter about their future summer selves.

Midday

Take note:
it is good to lean against a lamppost,
head back to contrast the coolness of the metal
with the February sun on your face.
Breathe.
Feel the pole shudder slightly in the wind.

Drifting off to Simon Armitage

(After seeing Simon Armitage speak about his writing process)

Water over rocks. My fingers slip, voices sink – and I am gone.
There are wooden panels, bound books.
Slow time, cradling the soft light
that sidles in through the iron wrought window.
These chinks of evening
that peek through the trees outside and slide in sleepily,
illuminated floor, chairs, poet, shelves.
My eyes lie down in the curve of the glass frames,
bask in end-of-day dreams, empty mind held
by the busy rustle of other people's thoughts
and the gentle murmur of the wind in the leaves outside.
From somewhere, deep within
the cosy balm of the background, a voice:
"I have nothing to say. Anything remotely interesting I think of
I try to fit into a poem."

Saved from Posterity

(Lincoln's Gettysburg Address was so brief the photographer didn't have time to photograph him)

I was too slow.
Unfocused as a misty morning
my camera box shut up, my tripod folded:
crouched like some hibernating creature.
So when this scruffy bit-of-fluff stood up
and started to set the world afire
I fumbled, suddenly an apprentice
embarrassed at the heels of my betters,
and in the time it took Lincoln
to carve a niche in men's hearts
I had not even prepared the slides.
I was too slow: I looked up at him
not dressed through a camera lens, but unclothed:
and so cheated history out of Gettysburg,
leaving the words to hang privately
in our hearts – a war medal to compare
years later, when all else was left for dead.
I was too slow,
and I am glad.

Faust at the Job Centre

Unthinking, not checking, being painfully human
he skimmed the bullet points, shrugged – and signed.
The next few years were absolutely fantastic:
Parties, drugs and rock and roll
sex from every page of the Kama Sutra
American Presidency, then on to better things.
A glittering career scattered with baubles
and broken hearts.
It was only after five or so years
that things began to get suspicious:
first it was the smell of sulphur everywhere
(in the toaster, the car, in then the shower)
and then it was the lumps.
Towards the end
he couldn't even get his hat on properly
and his shoes just wouldn't fit.
Tinted skin: the doctor diagnosed an all-over rash.
An unexplainable compulsion to gravitate towards farmyard tools.
It was only when he rifled through the admin drawer
and pored over the old, crumpled application
that he found it, hidden deep in the small print.
The devil was in the detail.

Oxford Issues

Tutorials
are intensive.
(Pause – think about it...)

Discussion groups
are useless.
Discuss.

Punting
enforces stereotypes –
and is encouraged.

Note taking
is too detailed.
[p. 20, line 17]

Tutors
are single minded.
Or are they...

Academic terms
are short.
(Unlike the lectures.)

Holidays
are long.
(– off)

Study work
is lonely.
What do you think?

Reading lists
are infinite.
End of.

Tutor's handwriting
is illegible.
Clearly.

Lecturers
avoid short, single
words.

Colleges
are partisan.
(Everyone thinks so.)

Set texts
are wordy.
Or, conversely, parsimonious?

Libraries
are all silent.
(Or so I've heard.)

Oxford
is confusing.
Definitely.

The Response of the Spherical Bastards

Astrologers are spherical bastards. No matter how you look at them they are just bastards.

Fritz Zwicky, discoverer of dark matter

Yes, but we're not all that bad Fritzy:
at least we're all 3D dickheads,
not those shallow, 2D circular bastards
that have no bloody depth.
And you shouldn't really blame us,
it's not our fault your horoscope is bad
and that you can't find love
simply because your stars aren't aligned.
Face up to it. It's science. (Well, kind of.)
Anyway, that's all rich coming from someone
who's supposedly discovered 'dark matter' –
what the fuck is that? Some filthy space version
of the Darknet – like porno for scientists?
It all sounds slightly racist, in our opinion.
You dirty old scientist with your greasy hair,
sweaty palms and your dodgy 'dark matter'.
We don't care what you call us anyway,
we're happy to be named spherical bastards
by someone who can't square up like a man
and accept his personally triangulated star sign.
Don't worry: we can just roll with the punches.

The Patience of Saxons

Banlocken
(bone locker, literally rib cage)
Herthcoffan
(heart box, a group of precious things)
Ferthlocken
(spirit locker, or a heart)
I have had these Saxons sitting on my desk
for years and years: quietly watching me
and waiting for just the right poem.
Alfred, Ceolwulf, Offa, Egbert:
their names smell of dirt and soil
and their words cling to me like smoke.
They will have to wait a while longer.

Quarantine Period

I want to go home.
I want to go home: I've had enough here,
force fed from feet to follicles
with facts, figures, with faces – these places,
unnatural acts of nature that build the spaces we breathe,
like grease on the skin, it works its way in
so you begin to think that the city won't leave:
that it won't leave you, that you can now never be purged.
This is why I want to go home.
I want to go home: I've had enough here,
this space, this substance, the very gloop and tannin of the town
staining the in, the out, the everywhere around,
because, well, being fed up has honestly just brought me down.
The sense of people not being where they want to be
geese autumn, here and gone like a magic trick: see
I mean, the sheer speed of things began to bug me so quickly
(ironic, I know) – but what's wrong with just being slow?
This is why I want to go home.
I want to go home: I've had enough here,
where the weight of the concrete
pools upwards through your shoes,
as if the city council had demolished the laws of physics
through some obscure bylaw
(to build a Tescos over it perhaps)
the tarmac filling your legs,
inch by ponderous, permeating inch
until the very street is inside you,
couldn't escape if you tried to,
dragging your legs, bending your head, pulling your spine
a blow-by-blow battle, creeping in below the belt, it's malign
and wanting to suck you, induct you,
to reach out and pluck you
out of your own belittled being into the endless city streets.
This is why I want to go home.

I want to go home: I've had enough here,
don't want to just "see how it goes", or to "play it by ear",
don't want to drown in crowds, I just want to- to disappear,
there one moment, then – puff! A plume of smoke,
my multi-coloured socks on the pavement,
and nothing else – except maybe a faint whiff of satisfaction.
And no one will notice. Because, unlike me,
they know what they're doing – they've got places to be.
This is why I want to go home.
I want to go home: I've had enough here,
this place. It's like – a broken piano,
keys slowly caving cavernously in,
wooden edges fraying, now wearing thin,
sky sinking down below roof level
notes falling away until there is one engine-hum drone
left running, alone; only a single sound to share,
empty soundscape laid bare
in the heavy, heaving mass of the city.
A single cowboy on the eye-stretching Wild West plains
developers have their eye on
for a new branch of Debenhams or maybe Costa –
it'd catch the commuters.
And look, I know this is all esoteric, overly poetic,
I get it: it sounds pathetic,
but honestly, to call it indescribable
doesn't describe it well enough
and I have to say something – I have to shout to be quiet
in this tangled knot of noise.
This is why I want to go home.
I want to go home: I've had enough here,
in this here-then-there-hurry-up-and-get-elsewhere life
this rush and race and dash of days,
my timespan sped up on some superlative spool
just so I can get to the end quicker
walls groping, absorbing me, hoarding me,
promising things will be slicker, all better, all bigger

it'll be fine if you just sink down and give in,
listen to the lulling laugh of traffic –
(the traffic, the traffic, listen to the traffic…)
No! I won't. I don't want to be a part of this – I want to go.
I want to leave, wash myself, scrub myself clean,
rub off the noises I've heard and the sights that I've seen,
scrape away all those multitudinous places I've been
jump up and escape out of the window and be far, far away
because, you know, I've done my time in this urban quarantine:
I want these streets to deplete, I need space to roam:
this, yes, this, is why I want to go home.

Twin Ambitions

One Place
Up. Up there, in the ethereal elsewhere of a dreamy sky
a swan. A nucleus compressed to a dot
by the clear cobalt around it, tight embrace,
held by the brilliant blue of a billion atoms as it follows
a current I cannot feel: and the world has let go
of all the clutter, the confusion, the chaos of life
scattering the floor in meaningless mess.
It has buried me forever in anchored material clouds. Up,
up there in the pure peace of an empty earth,
right up into space the swan floats,
basking, shrinking out of existence.

Another Place
Gazing lovingly down. My unreachable world,
line-littered map, every blue and green and brown
twisting like stationary smoke. Such beautiful patterns.
A dot, looking up at me, where I lie pinned
an insect on an endless, unendurable card of blue.
Watch him run, explore, live a life of a million things
glancing up at my exile in a prison of backwards gravity,
shut out on the wrong side of the elements
earth and sky, sky and earth. An oil slick on clean water.
The world retreats from beneath my grasp.

On Greed and Love

A tell-tale sign of love
is wishing that you'd thought of it first-
but being glad that they said it, not you.
So when you told me
that the word 'avarice' was lexically greedy –
crunching on consonants, snacking on syllables –
suddenly every other word took on a new meaning
and all the letters of the world
seemed to be telling me just one thing.

Autumn Winds

First day of October (any October, you choose):
down by the church, an Act of God,
the tiniest localised apocalypse the world
(or maybe the village) has ever seen.
Trees float off into the ether
so light are they now their leaves have fallen,
plastering the ground to create a future library
of shades, scuff-marks and skeletons.
Pluck an October (it doesn't matter which),
bringing the trailing nip of cold
nagging like a shopping list you left at home
dragging the wellies out and the spiders in
exchanging one brief clock-change-lie-in for evening darkness
and the ever predictable start of bloody Christmas shopping.
Pick an October (any October, go on),
they're all the same to me
there's nothing I can do, I can't stop

                        those leaves

                              from falling

Tuesday Morning

Look, if I could show you this path of birch trees
all bright on a Tuesday morning
I would; if I could I'd take a photo and bring it home for you,
pin it on the fridge. But I can't.
Because I did not mean to be here,
it was not where I was going – whilst I was busy living,
I just caught the earth growing – I saw it breathe. Still now, here,
talking to you, I can feel it inside me. In, out, in, out
like the inflected chatter of a robin high in a birch
by a path that was meant to be empty.

Haikus are quite hard

Haikus are quite hard –
the syllable count is tough.
Sometimes it goes over.

Crocodiles in Rome

Rain in Rome feels like seeing
a crocodile on the lawn:
not completely out of place,
but not really comfortable there either.
Umbrellas used for shade this morning struggle
under a surprise attack from above,
as if all the fountains had been rerouted
for an afternoon, or some ancient pendulum
buried deep under those scarred, sun-seared streets
had finally swung the other way.
I raise my face, letting the water wash down my cheeks.

Red Bush Tea

One sip, and I fall down the spout of the teapot of my past.
The heady brew of those few months, resting in the garden
after a hard morning's work in the woodshed.
Spring isn't awake yet and so we are wrapped up warm,
our paint-stained fingers tingling defiantly
as we hug the friendly curves of our mugs.
Out beyond the hedge, the mountains poke their heads up,
the Skirrid blinking, bleary eyed,
over to Hay Bluff and the Blorenge
whilst Garway Hill slowly ignites behind spidery cherry trees.
The scudding sky is breathless
with the weight of the heavy February air,
and it is just birdsong mirroring our wallowing, winding words
as we drag out the morning break over Red Bush tea.

Mapoholic

Ok, I'm going to just come out right now and say it:
I get great pleasure from looking at maps.
Not general, world ones: I'm not that far gone
I don't sit vacantly staring at an outlined – Lebanon
I mean *real* maps – the ones that uncover the world,
the adventure around you.
the come and go, the ebb and flow,
the to and fro of the roads I know
(and of those that I don't).
With a rambler's lust I trace
the smooth, sinuous curves of contours,
those lugubrious lines
that wash over the land as if it were underwater.
Trig points, bridleways, copses and lanes,
they bring me out in a cold sweat and ignite my itchy feet.
And the map key will kindly point out to me
the cattle grids and churches, the pubs and police stations
(which are suspiciously close together, I've noticed)
because can't you see with a key you can never be bored
hills, towns, woodlands all there, waiting, unexplored
I mean – did you know that Gower has a glacial fjord
(no, wait – sorry, that's Iceland)
it's like living in a toyshop –
Willy Wonka meets Ordinance Survey
it's there, it's yours. Reach out and take it!
Because how can it be anything but a joy to be here, alive
when we can sit and travel anywhere on a scale of 1:25?!
And the place names – oh, the names! – conjuring fleet upon fleet
of imagined idylls, sprung from words packed so tiny and neat
and anyway, how could one's life be truly complete
without knowing that there's a place near Monmouth
called What-The-Hell House?
I've always loved it – right from the start, day one
packing the car to go and spend a week in the sun

Mum'd say: "We're heading for Pembrokeshire – somewhere –
and I can't drive and map read." My dad would go: "yeah."
Cue my frantic waves: "Please! Please! Can I get us there?"
There was a 50:50 chance we'd end up in the right county.
Soon that wasn't enough. I needed bigger thrills
so I'd take off to the wilds, a localised Bear Grylls
armed with only my dog, a map and a book
to get out, to explore, to just take a look.
Because it's not a retreat into paper, it's a push into life
no need for order because our world is rife
with treasures, with wonders, a thundering cavalcade
of adventures and memories, just waiting to be made
because haven't you ever wondered
where that muddy track at the end of the road leads?
And if I'm honest, if I come clear
as the water that careers down in tumbling rivulets
into the Wye on the bare, heather-everywhere
slopes of the Welsh mountains,
the best thing about this map love affair,
the thing I wouldn't change at any cost,
is that though it lets me pluck places from thin air
I'm still gloriously, beautifully, hopelessly lost.

The Cow Factory

Come, let us go then, you and I
(take my hand, there, that's it)
to the place where they make the cows.
Mole-nosing, pressing up against the rusting fence
at the old loading bay, where bovines reverse and change gear
in the natural, nodding rhythm of working life.
Where machines once clanked, thistles now whir soundlessly
their pollen spinning in ethereal cogs and rivets, reaching up
to the rusty ducts and pipes swinging far above.
The ground has come full circle.
Like trees that bend to their roots the building burrows,
a great brick homing pigeon coming in to land.
Shattered window-eyes search slowly for the trees,
hermit-like bricks retreating shyly from mortar to dust.
Crumbling chimneys gaze longingly at the early morning mist
that whispers of the river rattle and rush of timelessness.
What was made here? The cows don't remember.
(Only calves now, you snigger.)
Then you turn away, and I follow, feet slipping in loose soil.
And the cows seem to know that even though we are leaving
the real work has still not yet begun.

Caught

I woke up this morning
only to find the house wrapped
gently, tenderly in cotton wool,
as if the morning was cradling us close
careful to catch us as we fell from sleep.

Night Walking for Wild Beasts

It is the kind of tree-infested black that lives
in the sluggish, silted seabed of your mind.
The footsteps I leave on the dark sink back in
like a palimpsest on the inside of my eyelid.
Ahead, the waterlogged path dives away
shining in the reflections of the moon,
a silver thread waiting for a Theseus to follow.
Not me. I tread on, hoof slipping as if reluctant
to obey orders. Even the lack of noise is black.
The sides of nothing pushing, matting on my fur,
a dense emptiness somehow shrinking to smother you.
Open claustrophobia. I can sense it behind me.
Then, suddenly, a hole in the world,
night retreating to reveal the stars in a puddle.
I gaze at the distance reflected up at me
and feel the weight of the horns on my head.

Stasis in Late April

Yes, of course I remember that afternoon out in the park,
that glorious, sun-dozed Saturday after lunch with friends
wandering out to the shops, laughing about
something or other. And then the picnic on the grass.
Air, hanging still between distant trees.
Cricketers. Children running. A kite. Sunlight.
There must have been sunbathers.
And the grass, pillowed beneath me.
I remember. I remember you.
Your laugh, your head on my chest;
our stillness. The way your fingers laced around mine.
Looking up and discovering the sky for the first time.

Autumn Somewhere Else

Through the open window, the skeletal leaves
scurry and crawl and squirm out of the open air.
Desperate to give one final, lifeless fish-flop and lie
staring up at me, pyre orange on windowsill white.

Mississippi on the Brain

Mississippi, you're a word I've heard that I adore
that I love to roll in my mouth like a pebble,
flick off my tongue like a rebuttal,
lay out lovingly on the windowsill,
river-mud oozing onto the floor.
Though you may look it
you're no specky-four-'i's, no Little Miss
but a great, swirling leviathan of linguistics,
your repetition is gorgeous, gorgeous
the hiss sound of your synapse-like sibilance
soothes us on your lexical banks
oh, you make me dippy, Mississippi.
Mississippi, you're an enigma, a code I just can't crack
currents running deep with your word-water secrets
you keep in between the H2O flow of your letters –
I just can't figure you out.
Crouching in my atlas, my dictionary, my head, some gremlin
on my shoulder that's grown up into a piece of poetry.
Listen: like the 'pi' you contain you go on forever, and
whenever you repeat you sound like a snake eating its tail,
Mississippi, Mississippi.
In your sounds I trace that groaning
great grey green greasy Limpopo-like river
down to the slow, black, crow-black, fishing-boat-bobbing sea
plagiarising to describe you, like the repetition that rolls free
when you bounce the word back from you to me, you to me
Mississippi, Mississippi.
And even when I've finished reading,
you leak through – an internal bleeding
I cannot stop: you seep, you stain,
your sound-sucker sticking to my brain
and I'm left mouthing, again again, that circular mantra
your round refrain, oh, you make me dippy,
Mississippi Mississippi, Mississippi.

Morning Mentality

Today I'm stuck:
today my feet are lodged in the ceiling
with my head hitting the floor
as I realise I left my crash helmet at home
today I am going to learn German,
word by word, the entire language
then move to France, and realise
I've picked up the wrong lingo
today I'm going to sit in the library
and work all day, read everything
then get in the cockpit and remember
I forgot to take the practical
today I will write pages and pages of poetry
before I realise my pen is empty
today I will go running and forget
my route, the shoes, my legs
today I will cook a dinner for fifteen
and then realise that I'm alone
today I will give a speech
to an empty room
and I will smile at the mirror.
Today I am stuck
feet in the ceiling, head hitting the floor
today I am stuck
but tomorrow I will do it properly.

The Mayfly's Explanation

Many wonder at his short life
and ask why he lives only a day;
well, after twenty-four hours just hanging about
he's buggered if he's going to stay.

The Woodpile

In the slow-go, wind-blow of the early November afternoon
I walk down to the woodshed, and begin to saw.
At first it is slow going. The trunks are lead under my hands,
branches unyielding to my push, pull, push, pull
a rocking horse tearing them limb from limb.
Then, gradually, it happens. I feel the bark beneath my grip
soften, dilate, until I am sawing backwards into myself.
I see the hours, spread like tree-rings, circling away from me
a screen on which I am played out, my words, my movements.
It is like my mind is being halved by the blade, I am spilling,
my thoughts, my memories, my ideas, pooling
in great lakes amongst the sawdust at my feet.
And then, suddenly, you are underneath the knife.
Like a magician, I have sawn you in half
(all stand please, cue rapturous applause)
and I probe, a tentative surgeon, with infinite care
amongst your innermost meanings, dating your tree rings.
I eke out your ragged imperfections, patching you up
(well, as carefully as I can with a hacksaw.)
And then you are branch again. And I am here,
neat, sliced logs halved at my feet
left feeling curiously whole.

After the Poet, the Bar

We talk the candle into submission
and then swap breaths over its dying cough.
And if we spat out poetry like phlegm
and extinguished the small light with our voices
we can leave knowing that we have just lit another.

Borderlands

The hill wears the road like a belt
fat forested belly sagging at the waist,
stretching the tarmac like elastic over the bloated land.
You can almost see gravity pulling at that huge mass
of elder and oak and ash and spruce and sapling,
the rotting limbs and the gnarled, slithering roots
and the pungent, all-over everywhere wild garlic
pressing it against the hedge in a bid for freedom.
The road's dashed white line is a no man's land:
a modern Hadrian's Wall stopping bark battalions,
guarding against rooted raiders that inch without moving,
that whisper voicelessly, counting time in falling leaves.
Not long, branches whisper to tired, cracked tarmac,
not long

An Evening in the Eagle & Child

A pompous first-year,
discussing Descartes and life.
An Oxfordmoron.

Landmarks

Every weekday, without fail, they walk past the shop window
gunpowder snaps popping like memories at their feet.
School kids, bored by decimals and drudgery –
laughing down Church Street, pushing mates,
crunching crisps and swaggering with weekend confidence.
Sharp crack, impulse, dash- a flashing energy
that whisks them away down into the cold plunge
of teenage years, the young crushes,
the slow, sad slip of friends once close,
now distant: until, barely audible,
the snaps that fizzed years ago
are dulled in those milding middle years
and onward into the gradual, grey days
that lie like the sea inevitably ahead.
Each weekday, outside the window
I hear the familiar pop and crackle
leaving ring-like ripples in my thoughts:
they permeate my memory,
sharp sparks of brilliance in the dullness of my mind.

Back to Pen and Paper

Letters, my love, I have longed for your dulcet tones
like a lemming dreams of Dover Cliffs.
How I tingle for your alphabetical arms
around my waist, rising, tightening round my neck;
your soft, sesquipedalian murmurings
have transmogrified me into a placid masochist
injecting injunctions and sniffing sentences.
Your allure and aphorisms
aid my attacks of alliteration addiction.
Ours is not the love of the tabloid journalist,
hacking and bending you to fit his large-print pleasure,
no, nor that of the politician, twisting you cruelly,
or the religious preacher, the primary school teacher,
the early-language learner, the Mills & Boon churner:
they let your fire expire on some bookish back-burner.
They do not feel your glorious anthropomorphic abuse,
your unstoppable, drowning murmurings, that I sense
Like ink in my skin as I sink, poisoned veins of verse.
I smile, willing myself under.
Now, perhaps, I can breathe.

The Other Poet

1: stirrings
It is past midnight.
It is past midnight, and I have gone to bed
and yet something else is still left here, going, ticking:
ghost writer, phantom typer,
I am a lie attached to a piece of paper.
I am not really here. Hello.

2: memories
Poolings. These breaks, quick gaps, a water-lapse
swift pauses and snatched restings in the river
as it runs, feet sore from its stony bed,
all the way from Plynlimon
that mountain on which no poem has ever stood-
the landscape defeats it, the earth simply eats it,
stanzas subsiding slowly into smooth syllabic silt
so that when you climb, you leave footprints in words
that could not reach the summit.
Let us watch from a safe distance,
put a good metre or two between us
and the end of the line.

3. dreams
It is past one
and I am dreaming upstairs.
Look, I can smell it – the sulphur of sleep,
the thousand tiny tugs at the soles of our waking lives
as the ground shifts and we fall down the rabbit hole
what the night time stole, the mind out on parole
down there it's blacker than Blaenavon coal (or so he thinks)
as he dances on synapses and jumps the wavelengths
of his innermost, down-dungeon mine shafts of mind, grasp
at the sides to slow your descent to the top.
It's past one, and I am dreaming upstairs
as I carry on writing.

4: the dreams of the other

In my nothingness, I dream
of Nothing.
How can it be anything else, when I am not here?
Nothing billows like nothingness, its bellows
in the haunted harangues of the night's hinterland
welling up in undergrounds springs
until my shoes are sodden, and I cannot feel anything
but the nothingness seeping into me.
To be empty, you must have been full to begin with
because Nothing is hard to get: you need to start somewhere.
Upstairs, I dream of something
of sea, of home, of phones, of TV stations, of biscuits
Of squash rackets, of chickens, of the sky,
of battered cardboard boxes
but here, I dream of nothing.
To reach there, I need to find something.

5: the steppings

It is past two
and out, about, up in the asteroid ether
of the black belted sky as it stretches over the hedges
as it wraps itself between the brambles
and floats with the willow seeds on the still water
out in the cold so alive it leaves blue bites on your ankles,
brushing your legs like stinging nettles in the long grass,
out there, somewhere, are the breakwater tidelines of paths
that wash muddily against root-buttressed banks.
Criss-cross, a catch-toss and splash-splosh
of night time ley lines, these spider web traces
on the back of the world's hand are empty
in the pulse-beat, dead of the dark.
Only the quiet wanders its signpost routes,
trailing skeleton leaves and snatches of owl-chatter
scenting fox-scuff and starlight-murmur
whispering into the boles of trees, filling the hollow air

loudly enough for no one quite to hear:
only to think they heard.
Leave the road, walk the fishing-net catch of holloways
that dart in shoals across the woods
these are the steppings, the stoppings, the walkings
of the night.

6: spillage

Having walked the nothingness into his shoes
and feeling it pool between his toes
he now finds himself drifting off course.
But being an other poet did he have anywhere to go?
First to be lost is the first person
slipping like an old gearbox straight through second
feel the gears complain, the fingers flex and spasm
then the stops all stop, an inverse spring
as letters shrink back into themselves
shapes all shrivelled and bent
he notices the punctuation has been vanishing fast
draining away between the edges of letters, the sides of syntax
he cannot be coherent, he is not in control, he is not even here
he is upstairs sleeping whilst the words run like ink
down the screen leave marks where they've been
and with the final splutter the rhyming dies
sentences curl up like spiders
then phrases dissolve
words go short
the last to go
last of all
words
last
la

7: drips [empty]

It is past three.
The page is running thin
whilst time stretches on until morning.
The other poet slumps on the keys involuntarily
asds-49i3ex.i]0Wa9] U3q3xi0'A3R,Q309cv
(before jerking back awake suddenly)
upstairs, I am sleeping.
The nothingness is drawing up my spine
as water does up litmus paper, creeping like ivy
mortar-crumble, stonecrack-tumble
a poem-wrecked jumble.
Nothing left but meaningless message
the breath of an intention
long lost in this black thicket of lines
a poet, wrapped close in his sleep
and a fading line of poem-prints
up the silty slopes of Plynlimon

Indigo Dreams Publishing Ltd
24, Forest Houses
Cookworthy Moor
Halwill
Beaworthy
Devon
EX21 5UU
www.indigodreams.co.uk